Are My Thoughts Keeping Me Fat?

Are My Thoughts Keeping Me Fat?

Learn how to get fit and healthy by changing your thoughts

Moe Sims

Copyright © Moe Sims All rights reserved

www.aremythoughtskeepingmefat.com
Follow on Twitter: @aremythoughts

No part of this book may be reproduced in any form or by any means including electronic, photocopying, recording or performed without the written permission of the author. For print or media interviews with Moneca, please contact thoughtskeepingmefat@gmail.com

ISBN 978-0-9896998-1-5

Thank you for your purchase . . . .

Legal Disclaimer

The information provided in this book is designed to provide helpful information on the subjects discussed. This book is not meant to be used, nor should it be used, to diagnose or treat any medical condition. For diagnosis or treatment of any medical problem, consult your own physician. The publisher and author are not responsible for any specific health needs that may require medical supervision and are not liable for any damages or negative consequences from any treatment, action, application or preparation, to any person reading or following the information in this book. References are provided for informational purposes only and do not constitute endorsement of any websites or other sources.

Table of Contents

Introduction
How much do you want to look and feel your best? 7

Chapter 1
My Story—Why This Book Exists 13

Chapter 2
Get Ready! How to Prepare for the Lifestyle Changes You Need to Make 19

Chapter 3
Write it! 31

Chapter 4
Start Now! Stop Procrastinating and Start Winning 34

Chapter 5
Top Nutritional Tips—My Secrets to Success and Health 44

Chapter 6
A Healthy Mind and Soul Health from Inside Out 58

Chapter 7
Sleep for Health—The Importance of Healthy Sleep Routines 64

Chapter 8
Incantations—Positive Affirmations for Success 67

INTRODUCTION

How much do you want to look and feel your best?

Most of us have a rough idea of what they need to do to be healthy and get in shape; everywhere you look there are books, magazines, classes, expert advice and exciting new trends focusing on the perfect approach.

However, in order to actually take the first step towards getting in shape, you first need the motivation to ACT—and that is where the challenge begins.

> *The journey of a thousand miles starts with a single step.*
>
> *Lao-Tzu*

I have written this book for two main reasons. The first is to give you the motivation and inspiration you need to ACT; helping you to take that first step on the journey to health and happiness. The second is to show you how you can achieve what you desire by monitoring and directing your thoughts in a positive direction.

By reading this book with an open mind, you are already taking that all-important first step; you can begin right now.

Remember—ACT

Ask yourself what you want

Create a plan

Tell yourself you can do it and believe

You are in control of everything you do. You probably don't feel like that you made a conscious choice to look or to feel the way you do, but you did. Failing to choose a different route, being carried away by life and not consciously making the decision to ACT in order to look and feel how you want to feel has brought you to where you are. By changing the direction you are travelling in, you can take control and be who you want to be.

How much do you want it?

If you want to be able to look into the mirror each day and see the person you strive to be, you need to work at it. A fitter, healthier you won't just happen.

Once you decide you want it, ask yourself how much you want it? It isn't enough to think that it would be nice to lose a few pounds, or that you wish you could manage to walk further, swim longer, dance better . . .

We all put things off, we all procrastinate and find reasons and excuses why this isn't the time to make the changes we know we should make. It's natural to feel worried about embarking on a journey or beginning a project—the fear of failure is very real. Instead of being anxious about the possibility of failing, tell yourself that if you never try you will never succeed. You can have what you want, if you want it enough. It will involve tough times, it will involve sacrifice, but if you truly believe that reaching your goal will be worth it, then you can't afford not to try. If this means you have to distance yourself from a particular food, lifestyle or person to reach this goal, so be it.

If you want it seriously enough, you will make time for it!

If you want it seriously enough you will pursue it regardless of previous failures!

If you want it seriously enough you will make sacrifices to obtain it!

So how much do you want it? It's time to have a talk with yourself about what is really important to you. Are you content with your life as it is? Is feeling good every day more important than that double cheeseburger? Most people will agree that having a healthier lifestyle, feeling better both physically and mentally, is the preferred choice. If you don't feel good about yourself, you don't feel confident, and you're less likely to feel like you have any control over your life—you won't feel like the person you want to be.

- ✓ Write down a list of thoughts that you can look back on to help boost your motivation—think about how you feel now and how you would feel if you achieved your health and fitness goals, keep them positive, focusing on what you want rather than what you are unhappy with, e.g. "I would love to climb the stairs without feeling out of breath", or "I have always dreamt of running a marathon."

_____
_____
_____
_____
_____
_____

In the end, you are the one who wins or loses, depending on the choices you make. You will only win back your confidence or improve how you feel by physically and mentally choosing to adopt a new lifestyle that will give you the results you want.

WHERE TO START?

Here's the secret to getting started: just start!

The key is to ACT now. Start from where you are! If you're having trouble starting a new program or plan, ask yourself a few questions:

> Am I willing to do what it takes?
> Do I believe I can do what it takes?
> Will it be worth it?

There are many times throughout our lives when our beliefs or thoughts are the very things that prevent us from taking action—we continue to ride the merry-go-round of ill health. Most people give up before they begin.

Lots of us tell ourselves, "I can't do this; my parents are overweight, my aunt and uncle are overweight . . . I will continue to follow in their path and also be overweight. Why am I fooling myself? Exercising and eating healthier is no use to me; I will stay fat."

I have come across many people who have similar despairing thoughts; they are missing out on what could be—what could change their lives forever—what could actually make them feel better about themselves! Continually dwelling on these types of thoughts becomes self-fulfilling prophecy—in essence, you are what you think.

> *We are what our thoughts have made us; so take care about what you think. Words are secondary. Thoughts live, they travel far.*
> — Swami Vivekananda

Follow me on the quest to become a healthier person. By reading my book I hope I can give you the strength you need to not only get started on a healthier lifestyle, but to continue with what will become your way of life. Dieting and working out alone are not the answer; a truly healthy lifestyle involves not just the body, but also the mind and the spirit.

By following a healthier diet, exercising and learning to calm the mind through meditation and other healthy thinking, you can't help but improve yourself.

So, let's get started!

CHAPTER 1

My Story—Why This Book Exists

So, you might be wondering what gives me the authority (or the inclination!) to write this book. What motivated me on my path to health and fitness? Well, there comes a day in almost everyone's life when the reality hits that it's time to make a change. One day, I too reached that point, just like you will in the future if you haven't already. My hope is that this book could be the catalyst that enables you to reach the same conclusions as I did when I finally realized I needed to make a change.

> *Physical fitness is not only one of the most important keys to a healthy body; it is the basis of dynamic and creative intellectual activity.*
> — *John F. Kennedy*

From childhood and all the way through to my sophomore year in college I was considered thin. I ate whatever I wanted without ever really worrying about gaining weight because my weight pretty much remained the same; it may have fluctuated between 2-3 pounds, but beyond that I was thin and healthy and I felt good about myself.

In fact, I was pretty sure I was invincible . . .

I figured that since I had always had a small frame, I would continue to be this way regardless of how much I ate. I assumed I was just "one of the lucky ones". However, unfortunately that was not to be the case. When I started attending college, I ate a lot of convenient fast food and lived a not-so-active life style.

In high school, I was active in sports. I enjoyed basketball and I loved track & field. I was a very busy and active person. In college, my focus turned more and more to school and spending time with my boyfriend who came to visit me nearly every weekend. My priorities had simply changed.

In the past I had also been motivated to exercise because I actually wanted to gain some weight. Believe it or not, I wanted a bigger butt—I thought it was too small! Anyhow, that wish came true . . . but with it came some other unwanted extras!

I now had a nice round butt, as well as a gut and a plump face. Ha! When I looked in the mirror, I thought I looked great. It wasn't until I saw pictures of myself, especially my face, that I thought, "Who is this person with this face?" My cheeks looked like squirrel cheeks stuffed with nuts. I was not pleased with myself . . .

"How did this happen?!"

I remember sitting on the couch, scratching the side of my waist and literally seeing a stretch mark appear before my eyes. I was outraged. "Why, what, when, how did I get to this point?" This was when I knew that something had to change. It was a turning point for me. The majority of my life I'd valued being healthy and fit, but suddenly I wasn't and *I didn't like it!*

That was my motivation to change my unhealthy ways.

But where would I start?

Well, the first thing I decided to do was purchase some tools that would help me shed the unwanted weight. I firmly believed that by shedding pounds, I would also be healthy and feel confident about myself once again. It wasn't just about losing weight, it was the whole package and I wanted it all!

I chose an exercise video package from an infomercial, which included an instructional video, a shaping bar, a measuring tape and tips on how to stay focused and be successful in reaching my health and fitness goals. I was so excited that I immediately ripped open the package the second it arrived and began the program that would surely make me look better.

I used the tools faithfully, exercising 1-2 times a week. The results were minimal so I decided to increase the frequency of my workouts. I started to exercise three times a week.

That was when I began to see my desired results.

I was dropping those unwanted pounds as well as starting to tone up just they way I imagined. It didn't happen overnight; it took dedication and determination. Getting the results I wanted required me to be persistent and consistent.

It hadn't taken a week for me to gain the weight; it certainly wasn't going to take just a week to get rid of it!

Increasing my exercise level was my own choice to speed up the results. You can take it as fast or as slow you want; either way, eventually you *will* see a difference. What it takes most is dedication.

In addition to working out, I changed my diet. I knew that all the good that came from exercise would have been diminished if I'd kept on eating the same junk and I was motivated to look and feel my best!

That motivation paid off, it made it possible for me to gradually eliminate eating pizza every weekend and helped me to start cooking healthy meals. I made easy swaps; I ate baked chicken instead of fried chicken and every meal included vegetables. If I ate out, I made it my priority to have vegetables included with my meal; my favorite meal was salmon, broccoli, and rice pilaf.

As my weight started dropping and my body began to tone up, my self-confidence increased.

I'd always had confidence, but not like this—I truly felt like I was winning—I was a winner! It was truly a wonderful feeling!

People complimented me on my new look and started asking for my advice for their own lives. They wanted to know what I was doing to become so healthy and look so much better, they asked me what they could do to make themselves look and feel as good.

Who was I to keep a secret?

My creed has always been to help others, and if I can, I will. So I shared my journey to better health with others. Many of the people I talked to seemed intrigued and even anxious to get the same results. I was excited for them and provided them with the valuable information that helped me; it is that same info that I am now putting into this book in the hope that more people can learn from my success and my mistakes.

Whatever advice I had to give to others, the point I most wanted to get across to them is that the thoughts we put into our heads are what will make us or break us.

Lifestyle choices and the way we think are so intertwined. We all know that modern lifestyles are to blame for the increase in obesity in the Western world. Obesity is a massive problem, and it is getting worse despite the fact that we are now more informed than ever about how to make the right food and exercise choices. The reason for this is that we need to think about what we put in our minds as well as our bodies.

In 2006, the Center for Disease Control stated that over 72 million Americans over the age of 20 were considered obese. Obesity is defined as a body mass index (BMI) score of 30 or more.

Think healthy, be healthy!

Here are some questions I would like you to think about.

Take a few minutes to write out your thoughts; it's not a test, so be honest with yourself—you are the one who matters and it won't benefit you if you lie to yourself.

- What motivates me? Have I reached my optimum health? If I pushed myself more could I obtain and quite possibly even surpass my goals?
- Do I believe that it's important to be healthy and fit in order to perform better throughout the day?
- Do I want to have more energy?
- Do I think that being healthier can provide me with more quality time (more outings) with family and friends?
- Do I believe that I can live longer just by eating healthier and incorporating more activity in my daily routine?
- What are some negative thoughts that frequently occur in my mind?

Chapter 2

Get Ready! How to Prepare for the Lifestyle Changes You Need to Make

It is a fact that changing your diet and incorporating exercise can reduce blood pressure, lower bad cholesterol, rid our body of unwanted fat and generally help us feel better and increase our confidence levels. Inevitably there are going to be things that hold you back, this chapter focuses on why you should make changes to your diet and exercise and looks at moving forward and getting past the negative thoughts that keep you from achieving your goals.

Failure to prepare is preparing to fail.

John Wooden

Escape Your Past

So maybe your family is overweight. You weren't brought up with a healthy diet. Your partner hates exercise. You couldn't run as a child. You hated sports at school. You've always been on the chunky side. You can't shift the extra pounds since having a baby . . . all of these things are reasons why it might be a little more difficult, but only because these things are in your head affecting your ability to get motivated and stay focused. You are not your family. You aren't even the person you were yesterday, let alone the person you were years ago. Your mind and your body are continually changing, you just have to direct that change in a positive way. Don't be a prisoner of your past.

Healthy Eating

Start to make changes by simply incorporating more fruit and vegetables into your diet. Any time you increase your intake of vegetables and fruits (and raw foods in general) you are doing your body a favor. Raw food is life for your body—it's nutritious, and low in calories and fat.

We are aware that vegetables are good for the body. However, when food is cooked some of the nutrients are lost. Therefore, eating raw vegetables versus cooked vegetables is preferred, in some instances. One serving of raw vegetables can contain up to 100 different phytochemicals. These chemical compounds have preventative properties that protect against disease. While cooking might destroy some of these phytochemicals, it can also augment others.

For instance, cruciferous vegetables like cabbage, kale and broccoli should be eaten both raw and cooked. Cooked broccoli has an enzyme called myrosinase that breaks down into sulforaphane, a compound that could prevent cancer and other diseases, according to Livestrong.com.

Cooking broccoli can destroy the myrosinase. But cooking it isn't going to destroy these vegetables, because once cooked, the compound *indole*, a phytonutrient that can fight pre-cancerous cells, is formed. The message is—get a good mix of both cooked and raw!

Drink more water. I can't stress this enough. If nothing else, drink, drink, drink water! It helps to move toxins out of your body. That alone can give you more energy and help you drop unwanted body fat. We should be drinking from a half-gallon to a gallon of water a day. A good way to tell if you are short on water intake is to look at your urine. If it is dark yellow, or orange, you need to drink more water. Your urine should be fairly clear, only a pale yellow.

Eating for Health

While you're striving to look better by shedding unwanted pounds, you are also helping your body prevent disease and stay stronger and healthier for longer. Vegetables and other healthy foods contain higher levels of phytochemicals, which are essential substances that increase the immune system's ability to fight diseases. With each healthy change you make, you are helping your body to fight against illness.

According to research, by eating fewer fatty foods and increasing our consumption of plant-based foods, we can potentially prevent certain cancers, as well as diabetes, heart disease, and Alzheimer's.

By eating foods filled with sugar and fat, we change the levels of our blood sugar, causing blood glucose levels to rise, which raises the risk of diabetes significantly.

By choosing to eat healthier foods, we are consuming fewer calories, upping our dietary fiber from fruits, vegetables and whole grains. Fiber helps the body feel fuller for longer, as well as making the digestive system work at its best so we can eliminate bloating, feeling uncomfortable and putting strain on the body.

Exercise

Exercise is the other essential element when it comes to feeling and looking better. The benefits of exercise are many, and there is so much more that a workout can offer you then simply burning calories. Exercise releases 'feel-good' chemicals in your brain, helping you feel better, boosting your confidence and even repressing your food cravings.

Exercising doesn't have to mean hitting the gym if that isn't something you enjoy. If you dread the gym, you won't be able to stay motivated and keep going, it will be too easy to give up. Find exercises that you love; maybe team sports are your thing, or you enjoy the freedom of a morning run or an evening jog. Perhaps long walks are the only exercise you feel you can manage; that's fine. Start there. In time you will be able to manage more and more and then you can try new things, always challenging yourself and pushing your fitness onwards and upwards.

Some people claim they cannot exercise due to other commitments; so make exercise part of your family life by including your family in your plans.

Walk together, kick a ball around or get active in whatever way best suits your unique family. Whatever your ability, there IS something you can do to get more active. Whether that means getting off the couch and walking around your own neighborhood or signing up to an intensive exercise class . . . as long as you are working at the top of your ability you will be pushing your fitness up and burning calories . . . and the sense of achievement and wellbeing is the amazing benefit you get to enjoy right away.

There's a reason why I repeat the words, 'just start now'.

It's a call to action.

If you continuously repeat those words in your mind, and you truly believe them, they can have a positive effect on you. By repeating these words you are using positive reinforcement and making those thoughts a reality.

Now, get up, choose your form of exercise (walking, swimming, etc.) and start slow. Then come back and read some more. I'll try my best to keep you motivated.

Growing up, I was accustomed to eating large portions of food. As I mentioned earlier, at this point in my life, I ate as much as I desired and I gained little to no weight. That was my experience until I hit my sophomore year of college. After I began to pack on the weight, a family member noticed and mentioned it. He jokingly said that I would be fat if I continued to eat unconsciously, as I had been.

I internalized some of what he said and at various times I replayed some of his words in my head.

I soon became aware of these thoughts and decided to use other thoughts to supersede the counterproductive ones.

My replacement thoughts were along these lines:

- "I will do the necessary things to ensure that I'm healthy and fit."
- "I will exercise and eat healthy, and I will obtain the body that I desire."

- "It is easy for me to accomplish my health and fitness goals, I just have to apply myself."
- "Power up!"

Positive Self Talk

Instead of saying "This will never work, I'm kidding myself," say "This will work and I will commit to it so that I will reach my healthy goals. I choose to be healthy regardless of my family's history."

Throughout the day say things like, "I will succeed," or "I can do anything I want." If you say it enough, it will happen. It may sound like a cliché, but there is power in positive thinking.

> *"As a single footstep will not make a path on the earth, so a single thought will not make a pathway in the mind. To make a deep physical path, we walk again and again. To make a deep mental path, we must think over and over the kind of thoughts we wish to dominate our lives."*
>
> — Henry David Thoreau

Everyone has different reasons for why they can't get started. They can't change their life styles, they don't have time now, they don't _____, or can't _____ or they feel_____. You fill in the blanks; we've all been there! The things we pound into our own heads, or the things we've always been taught, whether we have evidence or not, will be the things we tend to believe.

Sometimes what we were raised to believe is not how things really are. Family history doesn't always determine your destiny. It may be an indicator of what can possibly happen if you're not careful, but it's up to you to take the necessary steps to tip the scale in your favor.

A great example of this is found in the fascinating story of a lady named Annette Larkins. She has a family history of breast cancer. Her mother, grandmother, and several of her great aunts died of the disease.

Annette's aunt struggled with diabetes and had her toe and then her leg amputated before passing away. Annette deeply believes that if she had to depend on hereditary genes, she would not be alive because her mother passed away at forty-seven of breast cancer, her grandmother passed away at 36 of breast cancer, and her grandmother's sisters all passed away at early ages from breast cancer. She firmly believes that a change in lifestyle (eating, exercise etc.) has played a vital role in maintaining her good health at age seventy-two.

Annette didn't just give up and give in to the notion that she would follow in her family's footsteps.

Annette could have played the victim and accepted her 'destiny' but she didn't. She decided to become a vegetarian at a young age and later decided to eat all raw foods. As a result she's healthy, looks great, and is full of energy. Annette is seventy-two and has the body shape of a thirty-year-old! Overall she appears to be in her early fifties. She is reaping the many benefits of a healthy life instead of giving up and being resigned to what many would have considered an inevitable fate; proving that life really is what you make it.

So the question isn't 'can it happen?'—it's 'how can you make it happen?'

This quote from Annette's booklet, "Journey To Health," says it all—whatever problems you encounter can be overcome. They may make you change direction, they may slow you down, but they won't stop you unless you let them!

Determine your goal, find the necessary steps to achieve it, and though there will be obstacles, they are not insurmountable. If you have to crawl under, climb over, go around, or hit them smack in the middle, deal with them. Eventually victory will be yours.

When she says that victory will be yours, think about that . . . victory will be all yours because no-one can do this for you. It is by you, for you. To succeed you need to completely believe that you are worth it.

Things to Think About

It's essential that you monitor your thoughts!

Ask yourself;

- What are some of my recurring thoughts?
- Are these thoughts helping or hurting me?
- Are these thoughts pushing me to be better?
- What can I say now to encourage myself to reach my goals?
- Do I love myself?
- What are some things that I love about myself?

Don't be afraid to admit the things you love about yourself. Even if the things you love about yourself are centered on past successes; focus on these and work towards your future success with these in mind. Maybe you love your hands, your hair, your eyes, the way you help others, the support you give your family, your ability to cook . . . whatever you find in yourself to love can be turned around to make your goals so much easier to reach.

Base your progress on positives . . .

So . . . You want to lose weight because you love getting dressed up and going dancing so it would be great to look better in a new dress, not because you hate how your dancing shoes have become tight. You want to get fitter because you love how you used to play ball in the park and look forward to doing it again, not because you can't play ball now as you get out of breath.

It is okay to want to be healthier and more fit; however, it's also important not to beat yourself up in the process if this doesn't happen overnight. Don't be too quick to tell yourself you have failed.

Give it time!

Don't be too hard on yourself when you suffer a setback, or when things aren't progressing as fast as you want. Self-loathing is insidious—it prevents us from achieving what we want and/or need by making us believe that we don't deserve it for one reason or another.

It's a bad habit that many of us have without even realizing, buried deep in the subconscious. It results in exactly the opposite of positive self-talk, and we don't even know we are doing it!

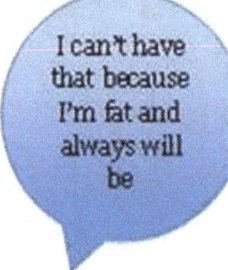 

Don't wallow in the pit of self-loathing!

Break the cycle. Think good things about yourself.

There is something good in all of us, so bring it out. Surely there's something that is unique and lovable about you. What is it that others like about you? What are your talents? What can you do that others wish they could?

Get into the habit of complimenting yourself and feeling good about it. The next time you look in the mirror, complement yourself on your hair, your eyes, or whatever, because you ARE beautiful, you just need to look for the beauty.

Many of us feel awkward or uncomfortable when we get a compliment. Accepting a compliment with good grace and appreciating it is a good way of changing how you feel about yourself.

Chapter 3

Write it!

What do you want to accomplish? Write it down.

Goals that are not written down are just wishes.

Fitzhugh Dodson

Sometimes just seeing your goals on paper makes you want to succeed at these goals. Now that you have them written down, look at them throughout the day or stick them to your refrigerator or your mirror so you see them regularly.

Studies show that those who write down their goals are more likely to accomplish them then those who don't write them down. Write your goals down now, then take action!

Include everything you want to achieve, don't be afraid and don't lose your nerve. Now is the time to admit what you really want.

One of the major pitfalls in goal-setting is to look at where you are and where you want to be, and leaving it at that. For example, if you weigh 250 pounds and you want to weigh 110, just writing down "I want to weigh 110 pounds" is not enough.

Set Milestones

Embarking on a program without any milestones will see you rapidly discouraged and naturally increases the likelihood that you'll fall off the wagon and go back to being a pizza-stuffed couch potato!

Break the goals down into sub-goals, with procedures for achieving each one. Be specific. So you want to lose 140 pounds. When do you want to reach that goal? Eighteen months? Okay, now, ask yourself what's halfway to losing 140 pounds? Seventy pounds? Great! What should be your target date for that? Nine months? Okay, what's halfway to that? Four and a half months? Thirty-five pounds? Break that down and it comes out to just under eight pounds per month. That's the goal.

> *First you write down your goal; your second job is to break down your goal into a series of steps, beginning with steps which are absurdly easy.*
> — Fitzhugh Dodson

Can you work hard enough and long enough to lose eight pounds? What will you need to do for that month? For each week of that month? Each day?

Now you don't just have a written wish; you have a plan.

Follow it! Make a detailed daily checklist.

As you start marking off the things that you accomplish, you will start to feel good. This act alone will provide you with the confidence to advance to the next level. This good energy and self-encouragement is essential to keep you going!

Don't just mark them off and forget about them; this is a daily practice and once you get into the habit, it will become your daily routine. If you forget one day, then go back to it right away as soon as you remember.

I tend to get really excited about my ideas and goals. In the past when great thoughts came to mind, I would tell myself that I could remember them. However, as the day progressed, I found myself trying to remember the thought, that wonderful idea that had occurred to me . . . and then realizing that I had completely forgotten it. This became frustrating—I was not accomplishing many goals and I was missing out on great ideas.

I knew something had to change.

I decided to make and record, on paper, my daily goals. This was very beneficial and when I did this, I noticed that I began completing 80-100 percent of the goals I had written down. I was impressed!

After that, I started to do the same thing for weekly, monthly, and yearly goals. The results were amazing. Instead of accomplishing 40-50 percent of my goals for the day, week, etc. I was now at 80-100 percent and I had a written record of what I had achieved—the sense of accomplishment when you can actually look at what you have done is fantastic!

CHAPTER 4

Start Now! Stop Procrastinating and Start Winning

- Do something daily so that you may obtain your goals.
- Take small steps.
- Don't try to win the race by sprinting.

It's important to consult with a physician before engaging in any exercise routine. Those with health issues such as heart disease, asthma/lung disease, diabetes etc., should definitely pay special attention to this. If you have any concerns, then ask an expert.

Easy Ways to Increase your Activity

While going to the store, instead of trying to get the closest parking spot, park farther away than usual. Carry bags to the car instead of using the cart. Take the stairs instead of the elevators or escalators. Also, find a fun way to increase your daily activity. Tennis, volleyball, skating, swimming, water aerobics, and pole fitness are some fun ways to exercise! Find exercises that you enjoy. If you just absolutely hate doing a particular exercise, find a fun activity that will work the same muscle groups or provide the same cardiovascular benefits.

Boredom or tedium is the enemy of progress. You might find after a steady routine of the same thing, that you just can't stand to do it anymore, or your fitness/weight loss seems to have leveled out far below your goals.

Continuous effort—not strength or intelligence—is the key to unlocking our potential.
Winston Churchill

To decrease your chances of reaching a plateau, change the order in which you perform exercises. For instance, if you walk one day, try working out on weights the next day. Also, gradually increase the intensity of your workouts. Try to go a little farther or a little longer each day.

When I exercise, I think of at least one of my goals, and that helps me push past what I thought to be my limit. Thinking about my goals while exercising helps me feel confident in my progress, and that my goals are within my grasp. It motivates me to push harder and to finish my workout session.

What is really stopping you from starting now? Do you have some fear that you may not accomplish your goals? Do you feel as though if you don't accomplish your goals you will be looked upon as a failure? Do you think the task is a dreadful one?

Our doubts are traitors and make us lose the good we oft might win, by fearing to attempt.
William Shakespeare

Those close to you may also be discouraging instead of encouraging. If this is the case then change that situation and surround yourself with people who are encouraging; people who will support you while you continue or embark on your journey.

Surround yourself with positive people who are willing to give you the support you need, and stay away from those who try to hold you back. People may hold you back or discourage you because they are jealous; really they wish they had the motivation to do what you are doing—so help them. Ask them to join you, even if it means telling them you would like their company. If they aren't interested and continue to undermine your own efforts, then perhaps they aren't the right people to include in your support network and you should move on.

Unfortunately, many people are like crabs in a bucket. Any crab experienced crab fisherman can tell you that if you catch one crab, you need to keep a lid on the bucket or it will escape. If you have two or more crabs, you can leave the lid off, because each time a crab tries to escape, the other crabs in the bucket will reach up and pull it back in.

> *People inspire you or they drain you—pick them wisely.*
> *Hans F Hansen*

Likewise, some people just can't bear the thought of someone else succeeding at something and will, consciously or unconsciously, undermine your efforts. You have to become one hundred percent confident in your goals regardless of what others say or do. Walt Disney used to bounce his ideas off of everyone in the office, and if everyone hated it, he 'went to work on it right away'. For this to work, you need to believe in yourself and your goals.

Find good support—it plays a key part in reaching goals. Surround yourself with people who enjoy your company and want to see you succeed, those with pure intentions.

It is very difficult to make a major lifestyle change all by yourself. You should be able to find support among your spouse, family, or friends. If not, try joining a group of people who share the same interests or hobbies (but not if junk food is your hobby!). We all need company and support.

Get out and meet some new people; attend networking events. Churches, civic groups, volunteer agencies—getting involved in any of these can help you have a positive outlook and increase the likelihood that you'll find someone who will encourage you on your journey. You will find yourself spending less time on the couch too!

People sincerely involved in some form of selfless service are generally less likely to be 'crabs in the bucket' and will generally have a more positive outlook on life. Maybe you can find someone who is looking for support as well. This way you can help each other. Seek out someone you can exercise with or talk to that will provide encouragement.

Accountability

Another important reason to develop a good support network is that you need to find someone to whom you can make yourself accountable. Knowing that you have to give regular progress reports to someone is highly motivating, even if only to avoid being embarrassed. You don't want to have to make lame excuses and disappoint someone who truly cares about your achievement. It is important you choose someone to be accountable to who is balanced and fair, supportive and who won't undermine you or overlook too many slip-ups. The most important factor when choosing someone to be accountable to is that they should care about you, so your goals are important to them, because you are important to them.

> *A friend should be one in whose understanding and virtue we can equally confide, and whose opinion we can value at once for its justness and its sincerity.*
> *Robert Hall*

I can't take all of the credit for where I am today.

Yes, of course, ultimately it's up to me to take action. However, there have been and still are people in my life who inspire me. They constantly tell me that I can do it. Just when I feel like my tank is running low and my goals are slipping away, someone reassures me that I will succeed if I just keep going. That in itself motivates me to put my best foot forward and continue!

Some may think they can do it all by themselves. However, if you do a little research or talk to some of the people who have succeeded in obtaining various goals, you will find out that there was a team behind them—family, friends, or colleagues.

You should aim to find people who;

- Understand your goals
- Believe in your ability
- Won't give up on you
- Won't pressure you too much
- Care about you in a genuine way
- Can listen to how you feel
- Make a mean salad (this one is optional! :)

Ask Yourself . . .

Who believes in me?

Who are some of the supportive people in my life?

Who do I feel able to open up to about my feelings?

How can I build up my support network?

Am I supportive of others in my life?

Can I identify anyone who may (intentionally or otherwise) try to undermine my efforts?

Have I been consistent?

What practical steps can I take to surround myself with more positive people?

Have I been under stress?

Inconsistency costs you time and can undo your good work. Too much stress can cause belly fat and hinder your health and fitness goals. It can also lead to slip-ups where you fall off the wagon and over-indulge once too often.

Everyone is different . . .

For some it may take 3 months to reach their goal, yet another may take 6 months or a year . . . depending on the goal you set, it may take many years.

Patience, persistence and perspiration make an unbeatable combination for success.

Napoleon Hill

Please be patient with yourself and try not to get results too fast by starving yourself or yo-yo dieting. Most of the time this approach to fast weight loss with fast results will only be a temporary improvement in how you look; it is not good for your health and in the end puts you back at square one, or in a worse position than where you started.

Fitness is a lifetime commitment; it should be approached as such and not as a get fit quick approach.

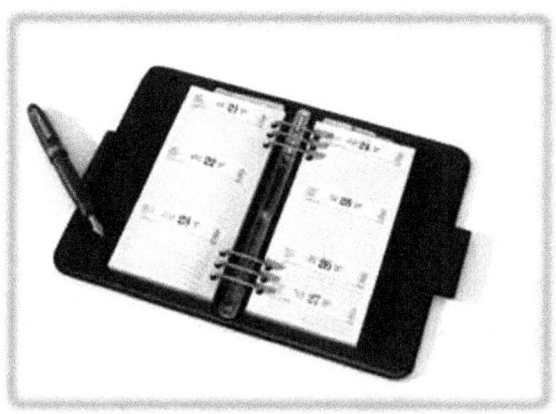

Revise your Goals and Persist!

If you don't reach a goal in the time frame that you initially thought you would, continue to strive for it. Give yourself additional time—adjust the date! It's not a race, it's a way of life you want to be with you always. That said, don't change your goals unless absolutely necessary. In other words, don't give up on one goal and work on another one just because you don't see results right away!

Be Honest with Yourself!

Sometimes it may be discouraging if you don't accomplish a goal exactly how or when you anticipated. That doesn't necessarily indicate that it isn't possible. Try adjusting the initial date set for obtaining the goal—sometimes you just have to be a little more realistic; the goal should still be such that it will stretch you and require effort but giving yourself a new goal can re-ignite your passion for achieving it.

Remember, it's better to shoot for the stars and drag your feet in the treetops, than to shoot for the treetops and drag your feet in the mud. Continue to pursue the goal; keep making progress! It could be that you just need to try a different approach.

When it's Torture!

Is your plan for reaching a goal full of nothing but nasty-tasting foods and painful, boring exercises? Are you torturing yourself because you think you deserve it? (It might help to review the section about self-loathing versus loving yourself). Make sure that the things you challenge yourself to do, if not completely pleasant (none of it is in the beginning!), will be tolerable and provide measurable results. Improvement to any degree is achievement, even if it's not 100% what you expected. Looking back at where you were versus where you are now should always be encouraging. If one way doesn't seem to work try another one.

The possibilities are endless!

If not now, when?! Your time is now. Don't let more time pass you by.

Sometimes something drastic needs to occur before action is taken. One of the undeniable truths of human nature is that change only takes place when the pain of staying the same exceeds the pain (or effort) of making the change. For me it was the pictures, the stretch mark, and the desire to be healthier. It's different for everyone. What's important is that you find the motivation and ACT! What will it take for you to make the change that will help you obtain your health and fitness goals?! You won't know unless you ACT now! Just think of all you can accomplish in a week/month/year if you take small steps and just start now.

Don't Procrastinate!

Most people talk themselves into waiting until tomorrow to start working on their health and fitness goals. Everyone has a different reason. Some say, "After Thanksgiving, or after Christmas . . . well, after the holidays, then I will start." What tends to happen is that the actual 'start' date gets pushed back and back until months have passed and in some cases years. In time, you forget about what you wanted and those goals are replaced by a sense of failure and dissatisfaction.

Ask Yourself . . .

Do you remember the last time you put something off? How did you feel?

Are you currently procrastinating when you know that you should have been done before now?

What can you do right now to stop that procrastination and move towards completing whatever it is you want to do?

How does it feel when you know you have completed a task in good time, without procrastinating over it?

How can you avoid putting things off in the future?

Chapter 5

Top Nutritional Tips—My Secrets to Success and Health

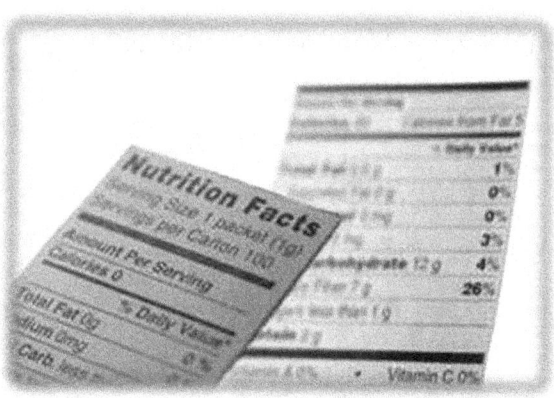

The following are nutritional tips and advice that has worked for me and/or others to boost the health and wellbeing. Please consult your physician before starting on any daily regimen or adding any supplement to your diet. Especially be sure not to over use any of the vitamins/supplements. Excessive use of anything, even if it's healthy, has the potential to cause undesirable effects. If you would like more research on any of these, consult a doctor or go online where there are many legitimate sites with information. As always, be careful not to take everything you read on the internet as absolute truth!

Starting or having a vitamin regime is very personal. Some people just take a multivitamin and think that's sufficient, but if you really want to know what your body needs, pay attention to it!

Do some reading to get started on your daily routine. Another thing we don't often take into account is that there is a right combination of vitamins and minerals that we need. For instance, if you live in a dark and dank climate, you may want to increase your dosage of Vitamin D, and get out in the sun when you can! Anyone who has worked a graveyard shift and been a day sleeper for any length of time will tell you how invigorating it is to get a day or two off and actually spend some waking time outdoors in daylight.

Those who find it difficult to get enough fresh fruit and vegetables may want to increase their intake of vitamins, and those who follow a meat free diet may benefit from getting additional iron.

There is so much to take into account when referring to the vitamins that you need. Listen to your body, do all the research you can on the subject, then decide for yourself, or with your physician or naturopath, what is right for you. Most nutrition experts agree that while taking vitamins as supplements are generally beneficial, the best way to get them is to eat foods that have high concentrations of the specific vitamins you need. Your body will process them much more efficiently and effectively if they are metabolized along with your food.

Wheat Grass is good for a natural boost of energy, as well as containing iron, calcium, magnesium, amino acids and vitamins A, C, and E. Spinach and broccoli in particular pack astounding concentrations of essential vitamins, including C, A, K, and several important B vitamins. Eaten raw they also provide dietary fiber and help stimulate weight loss. There are all-natural foods that contain fewer chemicals, oils and body scrubbers that will make your skin glow with health, and there is always plenty of water to drink . . .

Vitamin E

Vitamin E is found naturally in some foods, and has distinctive antioxidant properties. Antioxidants protect cells from free radicals, such as radiation and air pollution, which damage cells (this is why you might find your moisturizer or face cream is enriched with vitamin E) as well as contributing to a variety of ailments, including cancer and heart disease. This important vitamin is also involved with immune system functions. It is essential for healthy skin and good vision and eye health. Some doctors say that vitamin E should not be taken by someone with heart disease; others disagree—if you have heart problems, discuss your needs with the doctor who knows your case history best so they can advise you. As with all vitamins and minerals; these are potent and you should not take more than advised.

Sources of Vitamin E include;

- Vegetable oils such as sunflower oil, soybean and corn oils.
- Nuts such as almonds and hazelnuts
- Dark green leafy vegetables such as spinach and cabbage
- Fortified foods

Curcumin

One of the best things we can give our body today is Curcumin, a derivative of the herb Turmeric. The root and rootstock of Turmeric contains Curcumin, which is the active ingredient. Many people don't know of the power of this herb unless they are hit with cancer or another debilitating sickness and go on to research potential health boosting foods. Some researchers and proponents believe Turmeric could prevent and slow the growth of various types of cancer, particularly tumors of the esophagus, mouth, intestines, stomach, breast, and skin.

At the Cancer Treatment Centers of America it is given to patients as part of their complete Mind, Body, and Spirit program. Turmeric is also an anti-inflammatory herbal remedy and is said to produce fewer side effects than commonly used pain relievers. Some practitioners prescribe Curcumin for inflammation caused by pain and swelling or arthritis. Some even claim it interferes with the actions of some viruses, such as hepatitis and HIV. However skeptical you might be, it is worth some time looking into this amazing substance to assess for yourself if it could boost your health and wellbeing.

Vitamin D3

There is so much to be said for Vitamin D3. It is said to have fast become the new wonder supplement. We know vitamin D is the vitamin that we get from exposure to the sun and that without it the body suffers. This vitamin is important in so many ways that cancer treatment centers are suggesting high doses be given to patients. It should also be an integral part of everybody's daily routine because it provides bone health, aids in preventing cancer, and can help alleviate symptoms of major anxiety and depression from Seasonal Affective Disorder (SAD). Vitamin D3 is something that is often overlooked, but it really shouldn't be! I would suggest if you are interested in taking this important vitamin that you do some research first to assess how it could benefit you and how you can boost your intake from natural sources.

Sources of Vitamin D3 include;

- Cod Liver Oil
- Egg Yolks
- Fortified Foods

Flaxseed and Omega-3

According to the American Heart Association, 80 million Americans are affected by one or more types of heart disease.

Flaxseed is one of the richest sources of omega-3 fatty acid, (Alpha-linoleic). Since our diets rarely contain the amount we need for our overall health, it might not be a bad idea to supplement your diet with omega-3. With today's fast food, we tend to get more omega-6's than omega-3's, which is a big health concern. By eating more omega-3's we are doing our heart a favor by helping to prevent stroke and cancer. It also lowers the LDL or bad cholesterol.

Sources of Omega-3 include;

- Oily fish, such as mackerel and herring
- Nuts and seeds, for example walnuts

Vitamin C

Unlike fat-soluble vitamins like A and D, which generally have some dosage limits (though fairly high), it is literally impossible to overdose on Vitamin C. Vitamin C is water-soluble, meaning that whatever your body doesn't need will be eliminated from your body. Vitamin C is very effective at both preventing and fighting infections. Recent research has also indicated that Vitamin C in high concentrations injected directly into tumors is effective in fighting cancer, although more research is needed to corroborate these findings.

Sources of Vitamin C include;

- Oranges
- Bell Peppers
- Kiwi
- Strawberries
- Broccoli
- Potatoes
- Magnesium

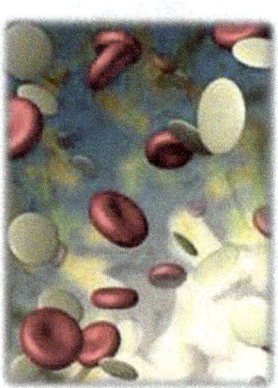

Magnesium is an essential mineral that the body requires to function. Most of the body's magnesium is within the bones but it is required for hundreds of chemical reactions in the body so it is important there is enough magnesium available. Women especially may be low n magnesium, and this can lead to a range of symptoms from muscle cramps and fatigue to more serious problems such as hypercalcemia, hyperkalemia, neurological and muscle disorders, hormone problems, insulin resistance and even heart failure.

Wheat Grass

Wheat grass can be grown at home, harvested regularly and added to your diet easily to provide a wide range of health boosting benefits.

Wheat grass is great for juicing or adding to smoothies, in fact many health stores serve shots of wheat grass as an energizing health boost. Wheat grass is believed to have a cleansing effect on the blood, reducing blood pressure and lowering cholesterol. Many of those who take wheatgrass regularly credit it with helping with weight loss and aiding in healing. This is because raw wheatgrass is a major source of powerful enzymes that the body needs to heal and be healthy.

Manuka Honey

Honey is a great sweetener and much better than artificial sweeteners or refined sugars so if you could find a way to use honey in your diet and to benefit from the honey as well, it would be a bonus, right?

Manuka honey allows you to do just that; with both antiviral and antibacterial properties that are more powerful and less easily destroyed than other types of honey, Manuka honey is more than your average delicious ingredient. It is amazing when it comes to healing wounds too, it provides a healing environment where bacteria cannot thrive so your skin can heal safely.

White Tea

White tea is packed with healthy antioxidants; it is the least processed of all the teas and as such has higher levels of antioxidants. This means that it provides the best protection against free radicals that damage DNA and accelerate the effects of the ageing process. It is also believed to improve blood pressure, cholesterol and promote healthy bones and skin, with advocates of this tasty, easy to drink beverage also claiming that it can work to prevent certain cancers.

Ginger

Ginger root has been used for hundreds of years as a medicine as well as being a tasty food flavoring and ingredient in its own right. The health benefits of ginger are many, and they include valuable medicinal properties such as the power to reduce inflammation, pain, respiratory problems and nausea. So for a range of temporary illness from joint pain to coughs to seasickness, ginger can help. It is also useful in dealing with more serious problems such as poor circulation. Many people believe it to have cancer fighting properties especially in fighting cancers of the colon and ovaries. By boosting the immune system, ginger not only fights illness, it also strengthens the body to prevent further illness. Get ginger from drinks or foods, add it fresh to meals or choose ginger snacks. The purer the ginger the better; enjoy!

Dangerous Substances

No how-to book about healthy habits would be complete without addressing the issue of tobacco, alcohol, and drugs, both legal and illegal.

The dangers of many of these substances are well-documented and yet so many of us feel trapped in a cycle of addiction or habit and continue to indulge in these habits. We all know the physical risks associated with smoking but official warnings can be surprisingly easy to ignore.

You have to think about the damage your smoking habit is doing to your self-image as well as to your body itself. How you see yourself has a huge impact on how you feel and this in turn affects your health. Most smokers will agree that smoking no longer has a positive impact on their life. But time forms habits, and habits can be difficult to break. The key to breaking the smoking habit lies in forming new habits that replace the smoking habit and then it is all down to perseverance.

Ask Yourself . . .

Do you feel guilty about your smoking habit?

Does your smoking worry other people in your life?

Is your smoking setting a bad example to the kids around you?

Do you ever feel self-conscious about the smell of smoke on your clothing or in your home or car?

Do you admire those who have quit?

Do you ever think about the money you would save if you quit?

If you could click your fingers and never crave a cigarette again, would you do it?

What steps could you take right now towards smoking less or stopping completely?

Do you have the willpower to quit?

Tips for Quitting

- Replace the smoking habit with a healthy habit—instead of smoking a cigarette, eat a piece of fruit, go for a walk or do something with your hands (knitting anyone?!)
- Exercise—use exercise to give you the boost of feel-good chemicals that you used to get from smoking. As your fitness improves, you won't want to hold yourself back with a smoker's cough or tightness in your chest. Exercise will help you notice these horrible side effects of smoking as they disappear and are replaced by a new vitality.
- Make yourself accountable—tell someone whose opinion you value that you are quitting so that during the weaker moments when you are tempted you have someone to talk to. Choose the right person; someone who you don't want to let down when you are feeling low.
- Don't give up. Many smokers give in and have a cigarette when they are trying to quit. Don't let a slip-up take you back into a habit. Instead, think about how close you were to quitting and get rid of the pack (never tell yourself you will finish this one pack than quit). Think about the smell on your clothes, what you could have bought instead and how disappointed your loved ones would be, not to mention the effect on your health. Then let go, forget the incident and move on with a new determination to quit. Think about it for a bit but don't beat yourself up. Make up for it with renewed vigor!

Alcohol

So, how about alcohol? We tend to get mixed messages about how bad, or good, alcohol can be for us. How much alcohol you consume is a very personal thing and it all comes down to how you feel about how much you drink. If you really care about your overall health, and are taking great pains to eat good food, exercise, and maintain a positive outlook, alcohol can undermine your efforts.

However, drinking to excess and drinking in moderation are two very different things and what is right for one is not right for another. One of the amazing things about being human is that we are all so different. The trick to true health and happiness is being honest enough with ourselves to identify what is truly best for us as individuals.

Think about your alcohol intake if;

- You regularly consume more than the recommended alcohol allowance
- You have felt out of control as a result of drinking alcohol
- The people around you have mentioned your alcohol intake
- You feel that you HAVE to have a drink in order to deal with certain things, for example social situations, drinking for "Dutch courage" etc.
- You feel it would be impossible to stop drinking completely
- You measure time by when you will next have a drink
- Your entire purpose when going out is to drink

The decision, of course, is yours to make. Only you can identify if you are drinking too much or if drinking at all has a negative impact on your life. Carefully weigh it up with a view to making an honest, guilt-free decision about your drinking habit. You may decide to stop completely, to cut down, or you may decide after careful consideration that you have a healthy relationship with alcohol. Whatever you decide, the key is honesty with yourself. Only then can you make a genuine decision after evaluating all the signs in your own life.

By identifying your relationship with substances and evaluating it, you can make a decision that is based on your own unique personality and mind-set. This is the only way you can make a choice and stick to it.

Changes to your lifestyle will only have the all-encompassing effect you want to achieve if you are prepared to make the change whole-heartedly, and this only comes as a result of being completely honest with yourself. It isn't easy to be this honest with yourself, but making a decision based on what you truly believe is much easier to stick to than doing something because you feel you 'should' or on another person's say so. And the sense of pride, achievement and wellbeing will be amazing once you have successfully made the change because it all came from inside of you.

CHAPTER 6

A Healthy Mind and Soul Health from Inside Out

We've talked about the physical things you can do—now let's focus a little more on the mental and spiritual aspects.

Immerse yourself in healthy things!

There are plenty of magazines out there devoted to making our lifestyles more fit and healthy. It can be fantastically beneficial to read about healthy eating and the benefits it can bring you. Sometimes just a simple article on a health-related topic can get you motivated to ACT now! You can also watch DVDs or videos on the internet that show various exercises and what they can do for you.

Additionally, take some time to quiet your mind. Think about the positive things that will result from reaching your goals. Stay hungry—not for cheeseburgers and pizza but for achievement and enlightenment. Recent studies have indicated that those who take the time for daily prayer or meditation are generally healthier and live more stress-free lives than those who do not, even those who are in characteristically high stress situations or professions.

> *Self-discipline, although difficult, and not always easy while combating negative emotions, should be a defensive measure. At least we will be able to prevent the advent of negative conduct dominated by negative emotion...once we develop this by familiarizing ourselves with it, along with mindfulness and conscientiousness, eventually that pattern and way of life will become a part of our own life.*
>
> *The Dalai Lama*

Whatever your beliefs might be, gaining control of your thoughts and actions is essential to self-discipline and success. You always want to work from a position of strength—inner strength.

We all have a range of different things we deal with on a daily basis. The more informed you become, the more likely it will be that you will stay on the path to a healthy lifestyle.

Keep in mind that your health and fitness journey should be one that continues throughout your lifetime.

The key is to love yourself; as you begin to achieve your goals, you will continue to take the necessary steps to preserve your body. You can make it happen, you just have to start . . .

NOW!

If you haven't already, fall in love with yourself. You're learning what works for your body and the more you strive to perfect it, the better you feel and look.

Love who you are, now!!

Do you ever say or think things like . . .

> If I was only 20 pounds lighter I would then love my body

> I was fitter, I would be more active and I would do more exciting things

> If I looked better, I would be able to go out and feel better about myself

Although these thoughts may not seem harmful, they may be the very thing that's holding you back from reaching your desired goals. The issue with thinking this way is that we begin to accept these thoughts as truth. This interrupts our self-encouragement and blocks our self-motivation, and eventually it keeps us from taking action towards having a healthier lifestyle.

Our thoughts often prevent us from acting.

Monitor Your Thoughts for One Day

What thoughts do you have that may be limiting or harmful, preventing you from reaching your goals?

- What effect do your negative thoughts have on your feelings?
- What effect do your positive thoughts have on your feelings?
- How often do you feel overwhelmed, stressed or angry?
- How could you think more positively and how would it affect your life?

All too often the problems we think we have or the things we assume others are thinking about us are all imaginary—imaginary problems thrive on attention. Stop feeding your imaginary problems and focus on real issues—the ones that have real solutions. The imaginary problems will dry up and blow away. Fall in love with your body, not someone else's body.

You are unique and that's what makes you who you are. We are not designed to look like everyone else; we are all individuals. I don't want to be like anyone but me. It's fine to admire another person's body, but don't desire it for yourself, because it can't happen.

What can happen is that you can feel good inside the body that you have by taking good care of it, so put your energy into taking the steps to getting into the best shape of your life! ACT now!

Just as you can find something good in the mirror and focus on it, find something beautiful inside yourself and make it the center of your attention.

Mindfulness

Mindfulness means being present in the moment rather than putting yourself on auto-pilot. The benefits of being self-aware and in the moment are many. This makes you feel more in control, helps you deal with stress and awakens you to the reality of your life and the world around you. By appreciating what is going on around you and refusing to be pushed along by the crowd, instead you will feel more able to listen to your own body and follow your own dreams. You can practice being more mindful in your day to day life to clear you mind of clutter and empower you to reach your goals.

Meditation and Breathing Exercises

Meditation is one of the most effective ways to relax and calm the body and mind. The benefits of meditation include a noticeable improvement in your ability to cope with stress. Stress and anxiety have a massive effect on physical health. Reducing stress has fantastic benefits for your health and wellbeing and there are many ways you can try to reduce the amount of stress you are exposed to, but we are all exposed to a certain amount of stress, at work and at home. What we can do, is to reduce the effect this stress has on us, by learning how to cope with it more effectively.

Through meditation, periods of quiet contemplation away from the distractions and demands of everyday life, and learning how to breathe in a more efficient way, we can all make a big change to our bodies and our minds.

Breathing

> *Feelings come and go like clouds in a windy sky. Conscious breathing is my anchor.*
>
> *Thich Nhat Hanh*

When we get stressed, people often say "take a deep breath!" or "count to 10!"

To make the best use of your breathing, learn to do these things the right way and you will reap the benefits of less stress, less anxiety, faster relaxation, better sleep and even more alertness and mental agility.

All too often we breathe in a shallow way; check your breathing right now. Are you breathing into your chest or into your stomach? It should feel like you are drawing breath deep into the stomach so that the diaphragm is raising rather than the chest. Breathe naturally, focusing on gently slowing your breathing and deepening it, never forcing it.

Breathing comes naturally, but good breathing can be learned, practiced and improved.

Self-Expression

> *Always be yourself, express yourself, have faith in yourself, do not go out and look for a successful personality and duplicate it.*
>
> *Bruce Lee*

Self-expression is important, and it can mean a range of things. Don't skip over this part because you don't think you are creative, expressive or artistic.

Self-expression isn't about being able to paint or sing; it is about expressing yourself in the way you feel most comfortable. That might mean an artistic activity, or it might mean simply making an effort to discuss your feelings with the people around you. If you find it tough to talk about how you feel, what you think or feel uncomfortable giving your opinion, you may feel powerless or frustrated. Take small steps towards becoming more open, or find a way to express yourself that doesn't involve others if you feel it would help; this might mean dancing around your home behind closed curtains! Whatever form your expression takes, indulge and enjoy it. Remember to give yourself credit for what you achieve and be proud of it.

Think about what you can do to express yourself more and note down some ideas. Try to come up with at least one way you can express yourself better in your everyday life and note down what you hope to achieve by doing so.

_____
_____
_____
_____
_____
_____
_____
_____

It is a common experience that a problem difficult at night is resolved in the morning after the committee of sleep has worked on it.

John Steinbeck

Chapter 7

Sleep for Health—The Importance of Healthy Sleep Routines

This is one of the most overlooked health issues in our society today. Being 'constantly on the go' is viewed as a badge of honor. Many of us put in long hours at work, we overdo it to get those promotions and move up the career ladder. The cost is often too high, however. Your body can't properly process the food you eat, nor recover from strenuous or stressful (physical and mental) activities without adequate rest. You need time to recharge, refresh, and repair. Your muscles, your bones, and your brain all need it. Proper sleep is like money in the bank—if you keep making withdrawals without making deposits, pretty soon you're running a deficit. You have to make those sleep deposits!

Loading up on coffee or so-called 'energy drinks' (which are just packed with sugar and caffeine and not much else) will only increase the stress on your body and reduce its ability to recharge itself effectively.

Some researchers have linked these beverages to increased risk of heart trouble. Research aside, common sense suggests they certainly won't add to your quality of life when you're already exhausted, and you should not depend on them to provide you with supposed energy that you can get much more effectively from proper nutrition and rest.

Sleep Deprivation

At best, sleep deprivation will lead to reduced cognitive abilities and a shorter attention span; at worst it can lead to severe depression and despondency (not to mention the very real risk of falling asleep while driving).

Find the optimum amount of sleep you need by going to bed at a reasonable hour without setting an alarm clock (best done on a weekend when you don't have to get up and go to work!). You might have to do it for a couple of days in a row, because if you're terribly sleep deprived, you may sleep ten or eleven hours the first time you try it. Sleeping too much can also leave you groggy, foggy, and, believe it or not, just wanting to sleep more; this is a result of the build-up of carbon dioxide in the body and can also leave you with a headache. Most people will function best with anywhere from seven to nine hours of sleep every night. Experiment with bedtimes and waking times to see what your optimum amount of sleep is, and once you find it, stick to it.

Sleep is the best meditation.

The Dalai Lama

When you can wake feeling refreshed instead of beating the snooze button to death or hibernating on your day off, you will have so much more energy with which to face the day—you will be recharged, refreshed, and repaired.

You'll be able to think clearly, and your outlook on life should improve as well.

Chapter 8

Incantations—Positive Affirmations for Success

We have seen how thoughts shape your mindset and in turn this governs your actions; in the same way, words that you speak make a big change to your inner voice and can encourage you to ACT.

Here are some positive self-talk mantras that you can use as they are, or change to reflect your own feelings. Just keep them positive and helpful.

When speaking these words do it with emotion. In doing so it is more likely that you "will it" into a reality.

Don't just say it, feel it and believe it!

- I am a winner and I will accomplish my health and fitness goals
- I love myself and I will do what makes my body feel good

- I love my body and I will give it what it needs to be healthy, and continue to be healthy
- I know that it's possible because I believe and I do what it takes to make it happen
- I will surround myself with loving and supportive people
- I will be supportive and loving when dealing with others
- I will be the change that I want to see
- I will use love in all situations
- I will monitor my thoughts because they can become a reality
- When I give I will give from a loving place and not just to get something in return
- I won't judge others because in doing so I'm judging myself
- I will love unconditionally
- I will start my day off by drinking water because I know this is good for my body
- I'm patient with myself because I know that I reach my goals with persistence and dedication
- I am passionate about my goals
- I am passionate about life
- If all else fails, I love
- I am what I eat so I choose to eat healthy
- If I don't meet a daily goal, I try again and continue to strive
- I understand that reaching my goals is a process, a journey, and I am patient with myself
- I have wonderful people in my life
- I exercise because I have goals and this helps me achieve them.
- When I exercise I feel like I can accomplish anything that is good for my body and my soul
- I will get enough rest to keep my mind and body functioning at peak efficiency.

Thank you for reading this book. I hope that you have found it to be informative and helpful. Now that you are done reading, what are you going to do?

ACT!

Get started now.

- Keep track of your progress, be persistent and consistent, return to any areas you need to work on; the learning process never ends.
- Keep pushing towards your goals, in time you will have your healthy body! Remember, obtaining or maintaining a healthy mind, body, and soul should be approached as a lifetime pursuit, not a once in a while adventure! ~ Healthy living is a lifestyle . . . Never give up!

Healthy Thoughts & a Healthy body starts with awesome links :)

To order copies of the book:

Call (720) 449-6877
email: Thoughtskeepingmefat@gmail.com

To instantly download the ebook, go to Amazon (http://amzn.to/QbANlF)
or www.aremythoughtskeepingmefat.com

Follow on Twitter: @aremythoughts

Create and maintain peace visit: www.deepakchopra.com

Detox & safely loose 10 pounds in seven days: http://bit.ly/1xutglJ

7 min workout: http://www.7-min.com/

Eat raw!!—Look and feel years youngerhttp://www.annettelarkins.com/

www.ingramcontent.com/pod-product-compliance
Lightning Source LLC
Chambersburg PA
CBHW051957290426
44110CB00015B/2280